Floods

LIBBY KOPONEN

Children's Press®
An Imprint of Scholastic Inc.
New York   Toronto   London   Auckland   Sydney
Mexico City   New Delhi   Hong Kong
Danbury, Connecticut

Content Consultant

K. Shafer Smith, Ph.D.
Associate Professor, Center for Atmosphere Ocean Science
Courant Institute of Mathematical Sciences
New York University
New York, NY

Library of Congress Cataloging-in-Publication Data

Koponen, Libby.
  Floods / by Libby Koponen.
      p. cm. -- (A true book)
  Includes index.
  ISBN-13: 978-0-531-16883-7 (lib. bdg.) 978-0-531-21351-3 (pbk.)
  ISBN-10: 0-531-16883-2 (lib. bdg.) 0-531-21351-X (pbk.)
  1. Floods--Juvenile literature. I. Title. II. Series.

  GB1399.K67 2009
  551.48'9--dc22   2008014785

Produced by Weldon Owen Education Inc.

3 4 5 6 7 8 9 10 R 18 17 16 15 14 13   62

Find the Truth!

Everything you are about to read is true *except* for one of the sentences on this page.

Which one is **TRUE**?

T or F Canals make flooding worse.

T or F After a flood, it may be hard to find water to drink.

Find the answers in this book

3

Contents

THE **BIG** TRUTH!

New Orleans

Food should be thrown away after it has come in contact with floodwaters.

John Watson, of Foley, Missouri, lived on his roof during the Midwest floods. He slept in a tent with many of his family's belongings.

CHAPTER 1

Water World

In the winter of 2008, snowfall in the northern Midwest of the United States reached record levels. Then, in early spring, heavy rains set in. As the snow melted and downpours continued, water surged into rivers. The rivers began to overflow. The region soon experienced its worst floods in 15 years.

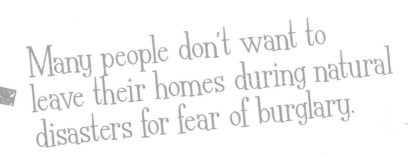

Many people don't want to leave their homes during natural disasters for fear of burglary.

Flooded Midwest States

Minnesota

Wisconsin

Michigan

Cedar River

Iowa

Illinois

Indiana

Missouri River

Missouri

Mississippi River

KEY

~~~ River

~~~ Main rivers causing flooding in the Midwest

---- State boundary

Flooded states

Raging Rivers

The Mississippi River, the Missouri River, and several of their **tributaries** swelled over their banks. Communities were threatened in seven states. Floods swept away houses and bridges. In Iowa, the Cedar River broke through its barriers. In the city of Cedar Rapids, one hundred city blocks were flooded.

Drowning Crops

The area that was hit by the 2008 flooding is known as the corn belt of the United States. Many crops drowned. Farmers lost millions of dollars in crops.

Farmers had other problems as well. Animals had to move to higher ground. Grain in flooded storage bins rotted if it couldn't be moved to a dry spot.

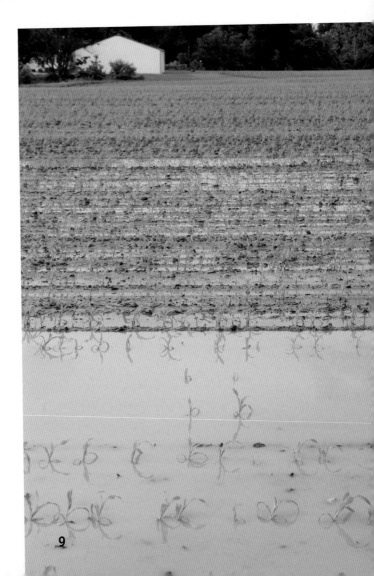

More than one million acres (400,000 hectares) of corn and soybean crops were ruined in the 2008 floods.

In 2008, Brandon Smith rescued his cats, Fry and Bender, from the flooding in Cedar Rapids.

CHAPTER 2

Why Floods Happen

Under most conditions, rainfall and snowmelt do not cause floods. Water is absorbed into the ground or flows into rivers and drains. In a flood, however, the water accumulates too quickly for the ground to absorb or for rivers and drains to carry. The excess water collects on the ground.

In Cedar Rapids, Iowa, about 24,000 people had to leave their homes.

Rain, Rain Everywhere

Most floods begin when there is a greater than usual amount of rain or melting snow and ice. Certain conditions make floods more likely. If the ground is frozen solid or dried hard from **drought**, it cannot absorb much water. So water levels rise. Some people know when to expect flooding. In some Asian countries, floods occur at the same time every year. They are caused by a wet weather system called a monsoon.

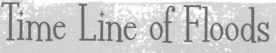

Time Line of Floods

1966

Venice, Italy, suffers a great flood. Thousands of people are trapped in their homes.

1998

Severe flooding in Bangladesh threatens the rare Bengal tiger.

Rising Rivers

There are three main kinds of floods. The 2008 Midwest floods were **alluvial**, or river-based, floods. These occur when water from rain, snow, or ice runs into a river and causes it to overflow. Mild alluvial flooding can leave behind **sediments**. Sediments help fertilize farmland. However, severe floods threaten lives, buildings, and farms near overflowing rivers.

2002 ➡

In Prague, in the Czech Republic, the 650-year-old Charles Bridge survives flooding. Some people believe eggs used in its mortar make it extra strong.

2008

After floods in New South Wales, Australia, some residents rely on supplies delivered by helicopter.

Coastal Floods

When sea levels rise due to storms or unusually high tides, coastal floods may occur. Powerful storms and hurricanes can create giant rushes of seawater. This seawater can flow far inland. Coastal floods are common in low-lying areas next to the sea. Southeast Brazil and the Gulf Coast of the United States often experience floods.

Paraty is a seaside town in Brazil. Slanted cobblestones move floodwater away from buildings.

Heavy rains can cause landslides, as well as floods. In 2004, about 350 people died in flash floods and landslides in the Philippines.

Flash Floods

A flash flood is a flood that builds up quickly. It is usually caused by heavy rain or a sudden event such as a bursting dam. A flash flood generally occurs within six hours of the onset of rain. Flash floods are very dangerous because they happen suddenly and are hard to predict.

Cars and mobile homes block Spring Creek, in Fort Collins, Colorado, after floods.

One Town's Story

The people of Fort Collins, Colorado, thought they were prepared for floods. The town had an overflow pond and an emergency center. Then, in July 1997, there was a series of thunderstorms over two days. This brought very heavy rain. In one part of Fort Collins, more than 10 inches (25 centimeters) of rain fell in less than six hours.

Streets turned into rivers. Rescue trucks got stuck. Cars floated away. Soon the overflow pond spilled over. Rushing water derailed a freight train. Trailers in two parks were badly flooded. Some trailers toppled over. In all, five people lost their lives in the flood.

Rescue workers search for missing people at one of the flooded trailer parks.

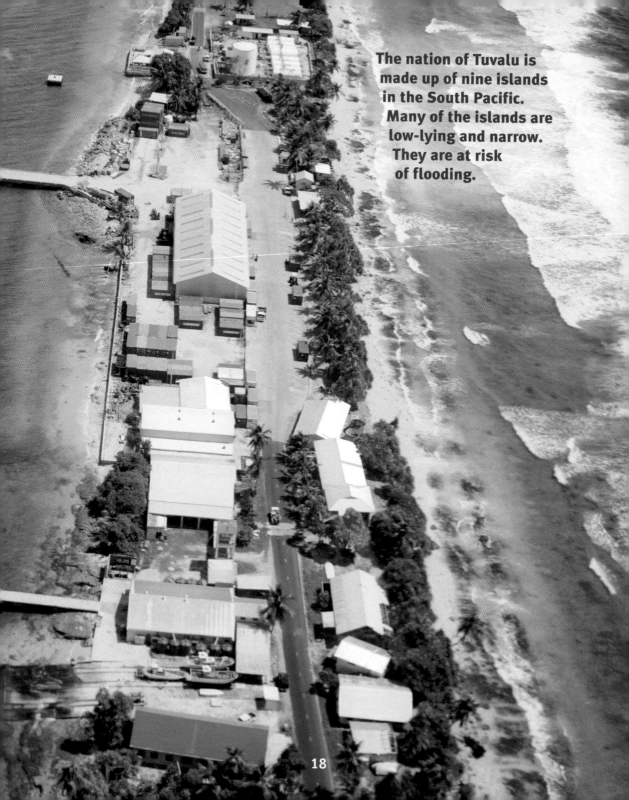

The nation of Tuvalu is made up of nine islands in the South Pacific. Many of the islands are low-lying and narrow. They are at risk of flooding.

CHAPTER 3

Living on the Edge

Most of the world's population lives near rivers or oceans. Throughout history, people settled where they could use boats for transportation. River water was used to drink and water crops. Now, the problem of flooding has become more serious in many of these areas. As the world's climate changes, storms are increasing and sea levels are rising.

Some parts of Tuvalu reach only 15 feet (4.5 meters) above sea level.

Today, Egypt's Nile River no longer floods regularly. A dam that generates electricity also controls the water flow.

Good for the Land

Flooding from a river or sea is not always bad. In Southeast Asia and China, farmers rely on monsoon rains and flooding to grow rice crops. Until the 1960s, the Nile River in Egypt regularly flooded its banks in spring. It deposited rich, damp soil on the farmland along the Nile. Since the Aswan High Dam started operation in 1968, the Nile no longer floods. Now farmers must **irrigate** and fertilize their fields.

Sinking City

Venice, Italy, is a seaport on the Adriatic Sea.
It is built on islands in a body of salty water
called a lagoon. Canals take the place of many
streets. Venice has survived for about 1,500 years.
Recently, flooding has become more common and
more severe. Special raised walkways
help people move about during
these floods. Today, scientists
are using Venice as a case study
to better understand the ebb
and flow of coastal waters.

Below Sea Level

Almost half of the Netherlands, in Europe, was once covered by water. The Dutch have been **reclaiming** land from the sea for hundreds of years. Part of the country was once seafloor or **wetlands**. In the past, windmills were used to pump away water. Today, electric pumps are used. More than 100 canals carry water away from the city of Amsterdam.

Parts of the city of Amsterdam, in the Netherlands, were built on reclaimed land.

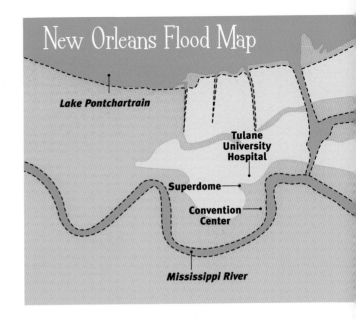

New Orleans Flood Map

Lake Pontchartrain

Tulane University Hospital

Superdome

Convention Center

Mississippi River

The city of New Orleans is nearly surrounded by water. This map shows how much of the city flooded in 2005.

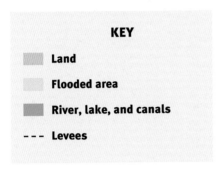

KEY

Land

Flooded area

River, lake, and canals

--- Levees

New Orleans, Louisiana, has always needed flood protection. It is situated mostly below sea level, on drained wetlands between the Mississippi River and Lake Pontchartrain. As in many places, human activity in New Orleans increased the flood risk. Wetlands take in water that would otherwise flood the land. Draining wetlands removes that protection. Still, no one was prepared for the terrible flooding that occurred in 2005. Years later, the city is still recovering.

Draining the Land

Marshlands, a type of wetlands, help soak up floodwater. Since 1930, more than a million acres (400,000 hectares) of marshland in southern Louisiana have been drained.

Losing the Coastline

The building of levees stopped natural sediments from being deposited at the river mouth. Without these deposits, the coastline began to erode, or wear away. This left less land to absorb the full force of a flood.

Floodwater Levels

Mississippi River

Katrina level

Normal level

Levee

Katrina flood level

New Orleans

Levee

Katrina level

Lake Pontchartrain

New Orleans

The city of New Orleans has drainage pumps and earthen barriers, called levees, to keep floodwater out of the city. However, during Hurricane Katrina in 2005, New Orleans experienced alluvial, coastal, and flash flooding all at once. The barriers burst for the first time. More than 1,000 people died and thousands more were left homeless. Many say that human activity has contributed to the disastrous flooding in two ways.

25

The state of Tabasco, in Mexico, is mostly an alluvial floodplain. In 2007, around 80 percent of the state flooded.

CHAPTER 4

Keeping Out the Water

The simplest way to avoid flood damage is to not live on a floodplain. However, many flat, flood-prone areas around the world make otherwise good sites for farms and towns. Flood preparation and protection measures are needed, especially as sea levels are rising worldwide.

Tabasco chilies take their name from Tabasco, Mexico. They grow well in its warm, damp climate.

Flood Barrier

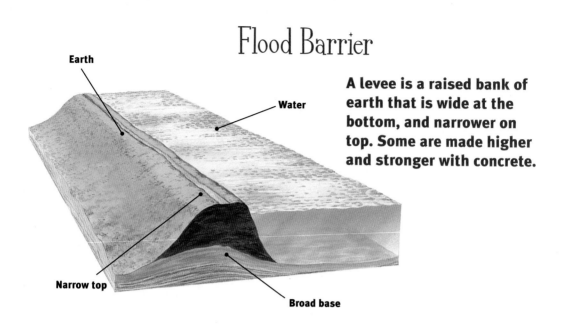

Earth

Water

Narrow top

Broad base

A levee is a raised bank of earth that is wide at the bottom, and narrower on top. Some are made higher and stronger with concrete.

Water Barriers

In places that flood frequently, people sometimes build barriers to keep water away. Levees are one of the oldest kinds of artificial flood barriers. A levee is a mound of earth or sandbags. These simple barriers are often effective. However, if too much water seeps into the base of a levee, some of the levee may wash away, resulting in flooding. Levees broke during Hurricane Katrina in New Orleans, leaving the city unprotected.

In the Netherlands, dikes are used to protect the land from flooding. Dikes are similar to levees. The country has thousands of miles of artificial dikes. Water is pumped out of areas inside the dikes to create extra land. The water is channeled into narrow waterways called canals. The tops of some dikes are used as roads.

In the Netherlands, water is pumped into canals such as this one. The water then flows to the sea.

The Maeslant Barrier is the world's largest moving structure.

It takes half an hour for the two doors of the barrier to close.

Shutting Out Water

Sometimes dikes and canals aren't enough to stop flooding. In 1953, the North Sea flooded the Netherlands. About 2,000 people died. The Dutch decided to build a series of dams and floodgates. In 1997, the Maeslant Barrier was built. It spans a channel about 1,180 feet (360 meters) wide. Its giant steel doors are usually open so that ships can come and go. But when the sea level rises dangerously high, the doors are closed.

Steel Gates

In England, the River Thames used to sometimes flood the city of London. Then, in the 1980s, the Thames Barrier was completed. It consists of a series of 10 gates. They are positioned end-to-end across the river. When not in use, the gates rest on the riverbed. If there is danger of flooding, the gates are rotated up into a vertical position. Together the gates form a wall facing against the tide.

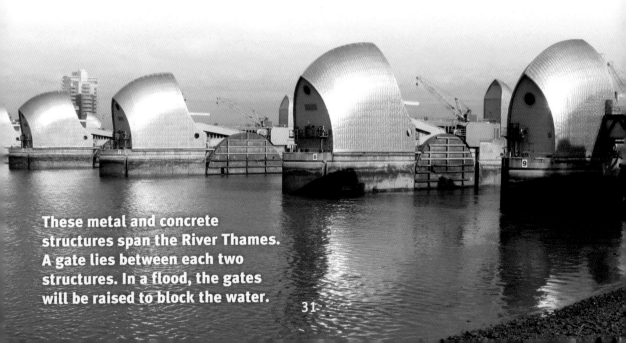

These metal and concrete structures span the River Thames. A gate lies between each two structures. In a flood, the gates will be raised to block the water.

In 2007, policemen in China helped emergency services rescue people trapped by flooding.

CHAPTER 5

Picking Up the Pieces

When attempts to keep water away from cities and towns are unsuccessful, the residents may need help. Often people are trapped and need help **evacuating**. Staying in a flooded environment can be deadly. The longer floodwaters remain, the greater the risk of **famine** and disease.

In 2007, more than 34 million people in China were affected by floods.

Clean Drinking Water

Surprisingly, one of the first things people need in flood areas is clean drinking water. Floods can cause drains to overflow, **contaminating** drinking water supplies. People can't drink floodwater because it may contain farm chemicals, fuel, and waste water. Germs that cause diseases, such as **cholera**, may also be in the water.

In 2000, during flooding in India, people pumped out fresh drinking water from a simple well called a tube well.

After Hurricane Katrina, many people lived in temporary shelters such as trailers. Three years later, many were still there.

Rebuilding Lives

After a flood, many people are left with no home, food, possessions, or money. It takes time to build new houses after a disaster. Survivors may have to live in temporary shelters for months, or even years. Architects around the world are experimenting with new kinds of shelters. These include small structures of bamboo, light metal, or plastic. It is hoped that they could be sent to disaster areas and assembled quickly.

People use sandbags to build barriers against flooding. In 2002, residents of Koenigsborn, Germany, helped build a sandbag barrier.

CHAPTER 6

Getting Ready

The more preparation people do for a flood, the less damage the floods are likely to cause. Authorities can do a lot to prepare. They can organize better prediction and warning systems. Better barriers, or more barriers, can be built. Emergency response plans, such as rescue by boat or helicopter, can be improved.

 Sandbags are practical because they can be brought in empty and filled with local sand or soil.

Scientists study the slopes of riverbanks and the soil around them to predict floods.

Predicting Floods

As early as 1441, a Korean king used a **rain gauge** to help predict floods. Today, scientists still measure rainfall to predict where floods are likely to occur. But modern scientists also consider factors such as how fast a river flows and the shape of its valley. They study patterns of ocean tides and currents. **Meteorologists** gather weather information that helps them predict the effects of storms. All of these things help scientists predict floods and issue accurate warnings.

Waterproof Rice

About three billion people in Asia depend on rice in their diet. Following floods in 1974, about a million people died when the rice crop failed. Although rice plants grow well in shallow water, they die if they are underwater for more than three or four days. Recently, scientists developed a new kind of rice plant that can live underwater for up to two weeks. It's now being grown in Asia.

In 2007, the River Severn flooded the city of Worcester, England. More than a thousand people fled their homes to avoid the floodwater.

Preparing for the Wet

In the summer of 2007, rivers all over Britain flooded. Drains overflowed, power went out, and water treatment systems failed. Roads and train tracks became impassable. Much of the land was affected by the flooding for weeks. Fortunately, the government was prepared.

Meteorologists worked with the fire service, the army, and other organizations to keep people safe. Warnings reached most of the flooded areas before the floods occurred. Most people and animals were evacuated in time.

Britain used both low-tech methods, such as sandbags, and high-tech methods to handle floodwater. One high-tech device used in many areas was the high-volume pump.

A high-volume pump can drain about 1,800 gallons (7,000 liters) of water a minute.

A Positive Future

All over the world, people are finding smart solutions to the problems of flooding. Although the number of floods in the world is increasing, fewer people die in floods today than ever before. More accurate predictions by scientists, quick response from rescue teams, and good planning all help save lives. ★

For centuries, people in Myanmar (formerly Burma), have built stilt houses to cope with regular flooding.

True Statistics

Height of floodwater that can knock a person off their feet: About 6 in. (15 cm.)

Height of floodwater that can sweep a car away: About 2 ft. (0.6 m.)

Percentage of U.S. flood deaths that occur inside vehicles: Almost 50 percent

Weather stations around the world: More than 10,000

First weather satellite sent into space: 1960, from Cape Canaveral, Florida

Highest level of the Cedar River in 2008 floods: More than 32 ft. (9.8 m.)

Did you find the truth?

F Canals make flooding worse.

T After a flood, it may be hard to find water to drink.

Resources

Books

Fine, Jil. *Floods* (High Interest Books). New York: Scholastic Inc., Children's Press, 2007

Ganeri, Anita. *Flood!* North Mankato, MN: Arcturus Pub, 2006

Oxlade, Chris. *Floods in Action* (Natural Disasters in Action). New York: Rosen Publishing Group, 2008

Scholastic Books. *Our Changing Planet: How Volcanoes, Earthquakes, Tsunamis, and Weather Shape Our Planet* (Scholastic Voyages of Discovery). New York: Scholastic Inc., 1996.

Spilsbury, Louise and Richard. *Raging Floods* (Awesome Forces of Nature). Chicago: Heinemann Library, 2003.

Woods, Michael and Mary B. *Floods* (Disasters Up Close). Minneapolis: Lerner Publications Company, 2007.

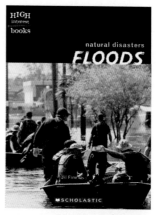

Organizations and Web Sites

U.S. Department of Homeland Security
www.fema.gov/hazard/flood/index.shtm
Find out more about floods in the United States, and how to protect yourself from them.

United States Environmental Protection Agency
www.epa.gov/globalwarming/kids
Read about climate, global warming, and flooding.

Nova Online: Flood!
www.pbs.org/wgbh/nova/flood
Learn about floods around the world.

Places to Visit

River Museum
350 East Third Street
Port of Dubuque, IA 52001
(563) 557 9545
www.mississippiriver
museum.com/
Look out for the flood simulation exhibit. Watch a flood in action and find out more about levees.

Water: H$_2$O=Life
A Touring Exhibition
www.ngwa.org/ngwref/
water_exhibit.aspx
The exhibit focuses on all sources of water. Visit the Web site to find out more about where the traveling exhibit will go next.

Important Words

alluvial (uh-LU-vee-uhl) – to do with flooding or deposits from a river or stream

cholera (KOL-ur-uh) – a disease often carried by water; cholera severely upsets the digestive system.

contaminate – to make dirty or unfit for use

drought (DROWT) – a long spell of very dry weather

evacuate – to leave a place because it may be too dangerous to stay there

famine – an extreme shortage of food

irrigate – to supply water by artificial means, such as channels

meteorologist – a scientist who studies weather

rain gauge (RAYN GAYJ) – an instrument for measuring the quantity of rain

reclaim – to drain land that was once too wet to live on, to make it usable

sediment – rocks, sand, or dirt that have been carried to a place by water or wind

tributary – a smaller river that is formed by breaking away from a bigger river

wetlands – an area of land that is mostly underwater

Index

Page numbers in **bold** indicate illustrations

About the Author

Libby Koponen is the author of other True Books, and *Blow Out the Moon*, a novel based on a true story about an American girl who goes to an English boarding school. Libby has a B.A. in History from Wheaton College and an M.F.A. in Writing from Brown University. She has traveled all over the world and ridden horses in every continent except Antarctica. She has never been in a flood, but remembers her grandmother telling her stories about floods her family lived through in North Dakota.